FAST FACT MATH

FAST FACT ADDITION

1 KITTEN
PLUS 2 KITTENS

1 + 2 =
3 TOTAL
KITTENS

BY JAGGER YOUSSEF

Gareth Stevens
PUBLISHING

Please visit our website, www.garethstevens.com. For a free color catalog of all our high-quality books, call toll free 1-800-542-2595 or fax 1-877-542-2596.

Library of Congress Cataloging-in-Publication Data

Names: Youssef, Jagger, author.
Title: Fast fact addition / Jagger Youssef.
Description: New York : Gareth Stevens Publishing, [2019] | Series: Fast fact math | Includes index.
Identifiers: LCCN 2017040521| ISBN 9781538219713 (library bound) | ISBN 9781538219737 (paperback) | ISBN 9781538219744 (6 pack)
Subjects: LCSH: Addition–Juvenile literature. | Mathematics–Juvenile literature.
Classification: LCC QA115 .Y68 2019 | DDC 513.2/11–dc23
LC record available at https://lccn.loc.gov/2017040521

First Edition

Published in 2019 by
Gareth Stevens Publishing
111 East 14th Street, Suite 349
New York, NY 10003

Copyright © 2019 Gareth Stevens Publishing

Designer: Sarah Liddell
Editor: Therese Shea

Photo credits: Cover, p. 1 (top) kuban_girl/Shutterstock.com; cover, pp. 1 (bottom left), 15 (kittens) Utekhina Anna/Shutterstock.com; cover, p. 1 (bottom right) Tsekhmister/Shutterstock.com; chalkboard background used throughout mexrix/Shutterstock.com; p. 5 Golden Pixels LLC/Shutterstock.com; p. 7 Africa Studio/Shutterstock.com; p. 9 Monkey Business Images/Shutterstock.com; p. 11 Hedrus/ Shutterstock.com; p. 13 (top) muzsy/Shutterstock.com; p. 13 (bottom) Vladimir Vasiltvich/ Shutterstock.com; p. 15 (puppies) cynoclub/Shutterstock.com; p. 15 (bunnies) Eric Isselee/ Shutterstock.com; p. 16 Celig/Shutterstock.com; p. 19 wavebreakmedia/Shutterstock.com; p. 21 Alohaflaminggo/Shutterstock.com.

Printed in the United States of America

CPSIA compliance information: Batch #CS18GS: For further information contact Gareth Stevens, New York, New York at 1-800-542-2595.

CONTENTS

Words in the glossary appear in **bold** type the first time they are used in the text.

ADDING ALL THE TIME

You might not realize it, but you add all the time. You can't escape math, even when you're not in school! Whether you're thinking about the number of plates to set on the table for dinner or counting out money to pay for a comic book, you're adding.

Math becomes easier to understand when you're using it every day in different ways. This book will teach you some "fast facts" of addition and show you how to apply them in your life. Are you ready?

MATH MANIA!

As you read this book, you'll be the master **mathematician**. Get ready to use your math skills. Look for the upside-down answers to check your work. Good luck!

YOU'VE PROBABLY BEEN ADDING FOR MANY YEARS. ALL YOU'VE LEARNED SO FAR WILL HELP YOU **TACKLE** SOME NEW IDEAS.

ADDITION WORDS

Here's a number sentence that shows the math operation of addition. You can also call it an addition sentence or an equation:

$$67 + 33 = 100$$

Mathematicians use certain words for the parts of an addition sentence.

ADDENDS $67 + 33 = 100$ SUM

MATH MANIA!

Look at the number sentence below. Which numbers are the addends? Which number is the sum?

$$10 + 15 = 25$$

Answer: 10 and 15 are the addends, 25 is the sum

JOIN THE FAMILY

FAST FACT: A fact family is a group of **related** number sentences that use the same numbers.

Here's an example of a fact family:

$$9 + 2 = 11$$
$$2 + 9 = 11$$
$$11 - 2 = 9$$
$$11 - 9 = 2$$

Once you know one fact in a family, you can figure out the others. Fact families are also helpful for **solving** problems with missing addends, such as:

$$2 + ? = 11$$

Check the fact family above. The missing number is 9!

MATH MANIA!

Fill in the missing addends in this fact family:

$$20 - 12 = 8$$
$$20 - 8 = 12$$
$$? + 12 = 20$$
$$? + 8 = 20$$

Answer: $8 + 12 = 20, 12 + 8 = 20$

JUST LIKE THE PEOPLE IN YOUR FAMILY ARE RELATED, THE NUMBERS IN A FACT FAMILY ARE RELATED. KNOWING ONE NUMBER SENTENCE IN A FACT FAMILY WILL HELP YOU UNDERSTAND THE OTHERS!

9

ALL ABOUT NOTHING

FAST FACT: Any number plus 0 equals the same number.

That makes sense when you think about it. Adding 0, or nothing, to something doesn't change anything! This idea is called the zero **property** of addition or the additive identity property. Let's try it:

$$15 + 0 = 15$$
$$125 + 0 = 125$$

The same is true if 0 comes first in the equation:

$$0 + 582 = 582$$
$$0 + 999 = 999$$

IF YOU ADDED 0, OR NO, ELEPHANTS TO THIS HERD OF ELEPHANTS, THE HERD'S NUMBER WOULD REMAIN THE SAME.

CHANGE IT AROUND

Let's see how this looks with two equations:

$$55 + 11 = 66$$
$$11 + 55 = 66$$

Both equal 66.

This idea is called the commutative property of addition. "Commute" means "to change." You can change the order of the addends without changing the sum. Let's try two more equations:

$$97 + 2 = 99$$
$$2 + 97 = 99$$

No matter which comes first, both equal 99.

MATH MANIA!

Use the photos and the commutative property of addition to solve the problem below:

Count the number of soccer players in each group. Add one group to the other. What's the sum? Now add the opposite way. What's the sum?

Answer: The sum of both equations is 7 soccer players.

YOU'LL ALWAYS GET THE SAME ANSWER, NO MATTER WHICH WAY YOU ADD TWO NUMBERS. THAT'S WHY THIS IS A PROPERTY OF MATH!

THE SAME SUM

Look at this equation:

$$10 + 20 + 30 = ?$$

Which numbers should you add first? The fast fact,

MATH MANIA! ◄

Use the photos and the associative property of addition to answer these questions:

Add the puppies and the kittens. Now add the rabbits. How many animals in all? Add the kittens and the rabbits. Now add the puppies. How many animals in all?

Answer: The sum of both equations is 9 animals.

WHICH WAY?

FAST FACT: The sum of two addends times a third number is equal to the sum of each addend times the third number.

This is called the distributive property. It states that you have a choice about how to solve a problem. You can add and then multiply, or multiply and then add. It's easy to understand when you look at an example:

$$2 \times (6 + 4) = ?$$

Check out the answer on the next page.

16

$$2 \times (6 + 4) = \text{?}$$

You can solve the equation by adding the numbers in the parentheses and then multiplying by 2:

Or, you can solve the equation by multiplying each of the addends by 2 and then adding the answers:

$$2 \times (6 + 4) = \text{?}$$
$$2 \times 10 = \text{?}$$

$$(2 \times 6) + (2 \times 4) = \text{?}$$
$$12 + 8 = \text{?}$$

$$20 = 20$$

YOU CAN SEE THAT BOTH WAYS OF SOLVING THIS PROBLEM GIVE US THE SAME SUM.

PARTY TIME WITH THE DISTRIBUTIVE PROPERTY

You're going to a birthday party for two friends. You get them both 2 gifts. One is $5. The other is $6. Here's your equation:

$$2 \times (\$5 + \$6) = ?$$

The distributive property says you can solve this problem two ways to find out how much you'll pay in all.

1) Add the numbers in the parentheses first. Then, multiply the sum:

$$2 \times (\$5 + \$6) = ?$$
$$2 \times \$11 = ?$$

2) Multiply each of the numbers in the parentheses by 2. Then, add:

$$2 \times (\$5 + \$6) = ?$$
$$(2 \times \$5) + (2 \times \$6) = ?$$

18

Solve the equation to find out how much you'll pay for the birthday gifts. The distributive property says that both sides have the same sum. What is that sum?

$$2 \times (\$5 + \$6) = (2 \times \$5) + (2 \times \$6)$$

Answer: $22

THE DISTRIBUTIVE PROPERTY IS A FANCY TERM THAT JUST MEANS THERE'S MORE THAN ONE WAY TO FIND AN ANSWER TO A PROBLEM! WHICH WAY DO YOU LIKE BEST?

PICK YOUR PROPERTY!

Knowledge of addition is required in every **career**. From astronauts adding **distances** in space to zoologists counting animal populations, these people use math every day, just like you.

You don't need to know the names of the properties of addition to know how they work. However, you'll be on your way to becoming a great mathematician—or another kind of math pro—if you do know them!

MATH MANIA!

Review the properties of addition. Match each equation on the left to the property on the right.

a. 9 + 6 = 6 + 9
b. 3 + 0 = 3
c. 4 x (12 + 5) = (4 x 12) + (4 x 5)
d. 10 + (3 + 2) = (10 + 3) + 2

1. associative property of addition
2. commutative property of addition
3. zero property of addition
4. distributive property

Answer: a. 2, b. 3, c. 4, d. 1

THE MORE YOU PRACTICE ADDITION PROBLEMS, THE FASTER YOU'LL ANSWER THEM. YOU'LL EVEN LEARN TO ADD IN YOUR HEAD!

GLOSSARY

career: a job that someone does for a long time

distance: the amount of space between two places or things

mathematician: a person who is very knowledgeable in mathematics

operation: a mathematical process (such as addition or multiplication) that is used for getting one number or set of numbers from others according to a rule

parenthesis: one of a pair of marks ( ) that are used around a word, phrase, sentence, or set of numbers. Its plural form is "parentheses."

property: a special feature of something

related: connected in some way

solve: to find the correct answer for

tackle: to deal with

FOR MORE INFORMATION

BOOKS

Marzollo, Jean. *Help Me Learn Addition*. New York, NY: Holiday House, 2012.

Zahn, Peter. *Let's Recycle: Represent and Solve Addition Problems*. New York, NY: Rosen Classroom, 2014.

WEBSITES

Fact Families
www.ixl.com/math/grade-2/fact-families
Practice fact families.

Properties of Addition
www.aaamath.com/pro74ax2.htm
Review the properties, and find out about other math ideas.

Properties of Addition
www.ixl.com/math/grade-3/properties-of-addition
Quiz yourself about the properties.

INDEX